Meditation Without Bullshit

Books by Black Swallowtail Publishing

Aaron S. Elias:

Meditation Without Bullshit: A Guide for Rational Men

Aaron Sleazy:

Minimal Game: The No-Nonsense Guide to Getting Girls

Club Game: The No-Nonsense Guide to Getting Girls in Clubs and Bars

Sleazy Stories: Confessions of an Infamous Modern Seducer of Women

Meditation Without Bullshit

A Guide for Rational Men

Aaron S. Elias

Black Swallowtail Publishing

Revision 1.0

ISBN 978-3-942017-05-3

To A. S. Y.

Contents

x

Preface

The popularity of the New Age movement can be easily explained by the natural aversion of the common herd towards critical thinking. However, for anyone with a rational bone in his body, anything coming out of that corner is of little appeal. In the case of meditation, this is an unfortunate state of affairs. Instead of throwing the baby out with the bathwater, this book attempts to present meditation in a clear and methodological manner that is suitable for everyone with a strong dislike of the spirituality business.

I have written this book primarily for men who are interested in meditation but not receptive to how meditation is commonly taught. This is precisely where I am coming from as well. I do not want to systematically exclude women, however. Quite the opposite is the case. Yet, I have found that women are a lot more tolerant towards fluffy spiritual concepts, no matter how far-fetched they may be. On the other hand, men seem to be easily put off when confronted with spiritual language, rituals that do not make much sense, or meditation gurus who are overly concerned with fostering a cult of personality.

My first encounter with meditation has been distinctly negative. As a teenager, I had come across video footage of a Japanese Zen monastery. I found it intriguing to learn that monks dedicate a very large part of their waking hours to meditation, with the goal of cultivating a clear mind. However, as I went through a few places that offered meditation in the city I was living in, I was exposed to a culture and worldview that seemed rather foreign, to put it mildly. I encountered cult-like group dynamics, people talking about chakras, the third eye, and the obvious need to donate money to keep their little cult group going. In one group, nobody was able to properly sit in the lotus position. In another, people ended the evening by going to a bar and getting drunk. In a third, it seemed meditation was merely an extended prelude to smoking weed and trying to hook up.

As off-putting as those encounters may have been, my personal experience with meditation has always been very positive. I quickly drew the conclusion that meditation is a viable way of learning how to lead a more focused life. Of course, this does not mean that you have to shed all worldly desires. My encounters with practitioners, on the other hand, could not have been more negative. I only met one group that was serious, incidentally in a monastery in the South of Germany. In order to stay afloat, they offered Zen retreats that were marketed to middle managers and executives. My encounters with the monks running that place were eye-opening. Seldom have I met people as serene as those. However, as I was unwilling to join the monastery, unable to pay for the expensive weekend courses they offered, and dissatisfied with the various spiritual groups I had easy access to, I had to find my own way.

At the time of writing, I have more than twenty years of practicing my own variant of meditation under my belt. I managed to reach an unusual level of calmness and detachment. People frequently remark how centered, calm and unfazed I appear. Mental clarity is rather beneficial indeed. In this book, I am going to share my personal practice, point out pitfalls I encountered, and provide you with a roadmap.

I am reluctant to put a label on my version of meditation. It is inspired by Zen meditation, zazen, but it is significantly less ritualistic. My initial exposure to meditation was via shikantaza, which is a variant of zazen. Yet, due to my highly analytical background, I stripped it of any resemblance of New Age thinking and superstitions. If you so will, you are welcome to refer to my school as *Meditation Without Bullshit*. Please excuse the profanity, but considering what people in the spirituality business hawk, bullshit is the most fitting description of it. I hope to rectify that situation to some degree with my book.

Aaron S. Elias

Acknowledgements

Many people have been directly or indirectly involved in the creation of this book. Ever since I first publicly spoke about meditation, which was about a decade ago, I noticed that there was significant interest. I thought it might make sense to write a book on my approach to meditation. Lack of spare time kept me from working on it for years. Yet, ever since I announced that I have been working on a draft of such a book, people kept emailing me. Thanks to you guys this book never slipped my mind.

I have had the opportunity to teach meditation, either in dedicated seminars or as part of teaching yoga. For the latter, I have likewise developed a stripped-down version that is much more akin to a relatively high-intensity bodyweight exercise routine. For about two years, I taught meditation in this setting. Thank you all for having been willing participants.

Others have been more directly involved. *Primus inter pares*, I thank Edward Cottrill for his extensive feedback. I also received helpful comments from Corley Atherton, Chris Griffith, and my lovely girlfriend A. S. Y.

Introduction

Meditation is an excellent method for relaxation. Its main benefit is mental clarity, which leads to a plethora of positive effects on your life. You can expect to become calmer, more relaxed, and more confident. All you need for meditation is a modest amount of spare time and a quiet place. Yet, meditation is commonly taught in a highly convoluted manner. It is for this very reason that *Meditation Without Bullshit* exists.

This book is the result of over two decades of personal practice. It is also the result of my deeply rooted skepticism. I stripped meditation of the nonsense this subject is all-too-often fraught with and present a version of it that is even more barebones than Zen meditation. The result is a school of meditation that should work perfectly well for anybody. Depending on your background, you may strongly object to how quickly I dismiss what many practitioners perceive to be fixtures of meditation. They are not! Just have an open mind, even if this means that you may need to reevaluate some of your positions. If you have fully bought into all the bells and whistles the spirituality industry sells, you may experience significant resistance to changing your opinions.

On the other hand, if you have had only fleeting exposure to meditation, then this book is an excellent introduction. It condenses my personal experience from meditating for over two decades. It also takes into account my experience from teaching meditation, either in dedicated seminars or in the context of yoga, of which I used to teach a stripped-down, no-nonsense version for several years. My classes concluded with the kind of meditation I describe in this book.

I have the impression that people generally enjoy getting introduced to my way of meditation. Frequently, my students asked me whether I could recommend books on that topic. Sadly, I could not. The books I knew were flawed in many regards. Some were written in a deliberately obtuse way. Others discussed things that do not exist at great length. As I could not find a book I could give to a rational person, I had to write my own.

Meditation Without Bullshit presents a straightforward and easy-to-follow approach to meditation. It is divided into two parts. The first part, Preliminaries, provides a quick outline of meditation, including its benefits. You will also get a first taste of meditation. The second part, Practice, has a much more applied focus and covers everything you need to know for proper meditation practice. In addition to discussing what you need to know, I also point out what you should disregard. My recommendation is to read this book sequentially. After finishing it, you may occasionally want to return to the second part. For the truly dedicated and ambitious I have added an appendix.

Lastly, I expect you to be a reasonably intelligent adult. This means that if you feel pain any point, then stop and consult a physician. In that case, you likely have much bigger issues to resolve than learning how to meditate.

4

Preliminaries

A Fresh Approach to Meditation

I am an autodidact. Therefore, I prefer figuring things out on my own, no matter if it takes longer than following the teachings of self-proclaimed gurus. Learning things that way often takes longer as you tend to make more mistakes, go down paths that lead nowhere, and have to figure out some elementary aspects on your own. On the plus side, you gain much more profound knowledge compared to just reading about something or adopting someone else's opinion without questioning or considering alternative points of view. You also tend to be a lot more critical about information that is presented to you when you explore an area on your own as opposed to being spoon-fed.

When I first discovered meditation in the zazen tradition, I was a fairly busy teenager. Looking for a shortcut, I explored the option of learning meditation from others. A common path with meditation is to join a Buddhist congregation or a similar group. Yet, I just could not see any advantage to all the bells and whistles those groups offered. There was no benefit to being part of a group. Standard props like incense sticks, candles, gongs, or even instrumental music I viewed as an unwelcome distraction. Worst of all, very few of the leaders of such groups seemed authoritative to me. Some particularly despicable ones viewed meditation as a means of filling their coffers or a convenient way of hitting on women.

It seemed that group efforts did a lot more harm than good. On the other hand, in the comfort of my home I can meditate whenever, however, and for however long I like. Giving that up for the doubtful experience of joining a Buddhist temple that is run by some New Age horndog was thus a highly unappealing trade. Factoring in the time it takes to get to the temple, it seems downright ludicrous to suggest joining one, considering that the total travel time of thirty or more minutes could instead be used for meditation right away. Those time savings are not the only reason why you will progress much faster on your own. Another reason is that you avoid needless distractions, which move you further away from your goal. For me, the prospect of meditating in a group was about as appealing as doing my homework in a study group full of underachievers. I don't think you will gain anything useful, in terms of meditation, from joining such a group.

The basics of meditation are quite simple. Just like with many other fields of human inquiry, however, there is far too much fluff being built around it. Practitioners are oftentimes all-too-eager to tell you about your chakras, the third eye on your forehead that you urgently need to open, or the inner child in you, which needs to be awakened. Scarily enough, more often than not, those people seem to believe all that mumbo-jumbo. You don't need any of that, though. What you instead need is a quiet place and a comfortable pair of pants. The old comfortable sweatpants you wear around the house when you are on your own will do just fine. You don't even need a pillow.

Being a skeptic, I never bought into the promises of the New Age industry surrounding the various schools of meditation and instead went straight to the core of meditation. The core of meditation comes with some difficulty, though. The initial difficulty is sitting in the lotus position, which is depicted in the figure below. I will talk about it in detail later. I will also present alternatives as well as a natural progression to help you get closer to being able to sit in that position. Sitting in the lotus position is not easy. I was able to sit in the lotus right away, as my body is limber. Yet, sitting comfortably in the lotus position for a longer amount of

Figure 1: The Lotus Position

time took me months of practice. As challenging as sitting in the lotus position may be, it is nothing compared to dealing with all the thoughts that start to enter your mind once all sources of distraction are removed.

It is challenging to learn to meditate in the Zen tradition or related ones. Other schools promise similar effects while removing the hurdles, but you cannot dilute something and maintain the same quality. Consequently, seemingly more approachable schools of meditation only waste your time. Let me just highlight one very popular approach to meditation, namely guided meditation. This means that you listen to an audio recording or the words of a meditation teacher as you conjure up images in your mind corresponding to whatever you hear. Instead of sitting in the lotus position, you sit on a chair or possibly even lie down. The content of such guided meditations is clichéd, with no shortage of open fields, cold breezes, clear waterfronts, and bright skies. All those images are superficial means to make you relax by evoking associations. By imagining certain sceneries and events you keep your mind occupied, but this is the exact opposite of what you can achieve through meditation, which is learning to actively control your mind and your thoughts.

If you learnt to control your thoughts you would not have any need for guided meditations. Chanting serves a similar purpose, but this may not be obvious. You do not need to bother with it either. My view is that those approaches are red herrings that will do nothing positive for you in the long run. Through meditation in a more traditional manner, such as what I outline in this book, you will be able to reach much deeper meditative states. This will allow you to relax at a level that you will find impossible to achieve by following a guided meditation.

The Long Path Ahead

Earlier, I briefly alluded to some of the positive effects meditation might have on your life. I hopefully have not given you the impression that it will be easy to get to the point where you will be able to reap all those benefits. To provide you with a more realistic perspective, I am therefore going to outline the required effort. To be perfectly clear, the issue is not so much the amount of time you need to spend every day. It is about consistent practice. Improving your mental health through meditation should be within reach for most of you, but you need to make, at the very least, a modest daily sacrifice. Presumably, you brush and floss your teeth every day, so maybe it will help you to view meditation as a procedure akin to flossing your mind.

The main hurdle you will face is that it may prove

difficult to handle all the thoughts that keep crop-ping up while meditating. You will gradually get used to it. However, the first few times will indeed be very challenging as they lead to experiences you may be completely unfamiliar with. To ease the transition into a meditative lifestyle, I suggest two-minute meditations in the beginning, which we will quickly extend to five minutes. Only after you are able to endure that without any problems will we extend the time limit. I chose such a short amount of time to lower the barrier of entry. We will have increasingly longer sessions once you have become comfortable with those durations.

You will probably be able to reap a good eighty to ninety percent of the benefits of meditation with a modest investment of time consisting of ten to fifteen minutes a day. Yes, of course, I am pulling those numbers out of thin air. Still, the point is that diminishing returns kick in quickly. Keep in mind that this statement is coming from someone who has meditated for one to two hours a day many hundreds of times. On that note, meditating for one to two hours a day is far from the limit. Zen monks spend most of their waking day sitting in the lotus position. At my most extreme, I spent five to six hours a day meditating, but I eventually realized that I was overdoing it, not in the least be-cause my desire to push my limits in the field of meditation began to impinge on other areas of my life. For years, my daily regimen has been much more manageable. Normally I meditate for half an hour or less. Just try it and decide for yourself how far you want to go. You will probably find that by meditating for fifteen minutes a day the quality of your life already improves noticeably. Even if you never go beyond that, you can expect to benefit significantly from meditation.

Again, do not expect quick fixes. Even though you may consider yourself a balanced and stable person, that perception may be wrong. For instance, only after I started meditating did I become aware of the incredible amount of distractions surrounding us. There is traffic noise, radio, television, your computer, the constant lure of your smartphone, and the list goes on and on. I am not merely talking about audible noise. There are also distractions due to information overload. The consequence is that we are hardly ever on our own and alone with our thoughts. Some of you may not even know what it feels like to think about something for a prolonged period of time.

You are probably not even aware of all the noise because you assume it to be normal and you have learnt to live with it. Feel free to put this book down for a minute or two and reflect on your surroundings. Is there peace and quiet or is something distracting you? This could be music, your TV, a wall clock, or noise caused by other people. Try to identify as many sources as you can and keep in mind that any kind of distraction may affect your mental health negatively. You may not even know what it feels like to be without distractions and feel discomfort once you are in a situation where the distractions you are used to are temporarily gone. Those situations are rare, but maybe you have had the experience of a blackout while you were alone at home. Without electricity in your home, did you panic or did you just sit there, knowing or hoping that the problem will be fixed soon? To give you a heads-up: meditation will put you in a similar situation as you will deliberately exclude distractions. As a consequence, you will learn that your mind, when left to its own devices, is a lot more restless than you are aware of. With meditation, we are going to work on that problem.

Benefits of Meditation

As a busy person, you may legitimately ask yourself why you should bother with meditation. I think that meditation is one of the most efficient uses of your time. Your daily investment may be as little as a few minutes on the low end. With just fifteen minutes per day, you will reap significant benefits over the long run. Meditating for longer intervals quickly reaches the region of diminishing returns. After all, your spare time is limited. There is the alternative of going all in and joining a monastery. This might maximize your physical well-being but comes at the expense of having to live a life of relative poverty. I am not overly concerned with extremes, however. Instead, I want to highlight how you can benefit from meditation with just a little bit of your spare time, which should be possible even if you were the busiest among my readers.

First and foremost, meditation is a great way to relax. As long as you do not aim to push your physical limits but instead meditate for a manageable amount of time, there are only positive sides to it. So, let me tell you more about some of the spillover effects that will positively influence your everyday life. In this chapter, I highlight common occurrences in daily life and how the positive effects of meditation may help you handle them better.

In a nutshell, meditation is a wonderful tool for calming a restless mind. What is more, you may greatly underestimate how restless your mind is when it is left to its own devices. This is particularly true if you are caught in the rat race and neglect to evaluate how your life is going. That is an easy trap to fall into, considering that the next rung on the ladder is always in sight.

Confidence

One of the consequences of regular meditation is that it will make you appear calm and collected. What would you think if you saw someone like that — wouldn't you assume he was experienced, secure about himself and his actions, as well as confident? The fact that people often make unfounded assumptions about confidence became blatantly obvious to me after entering university. I had been meditating for a few years already and my academic record was good. However, I was not the most confident person around. To my great surprise, though, some of my fellow students made assumptions that had little grounding in reality. I did not talk a lot, but when I bothered to contribute something to class or to discussions outside the classroom, it was something worth listening to. In addition, I did not exhibit nervous ticks, which only confirmed their opinion. Without even wanting it, I was encouraged to take positions of responsibility and I won the vote for some admittedly minor roles. Yet, those were decisions by vote, which means that I appeared to be the most capable candidate.

Those are just anecdotes, but they draw your attention to a few important points. One is that it does not matter how insecure you feel. It is more important how you appear to others. Meditation will help you in that regard as it will make you appear much calmer. You don't even have to demonstrate a lot of competence in many areas either. Obviously, bluffing your way through a class on Multivariate Calculus is infinitely more difficult than doing the same in Introduction to Gender Studies, but you get the idea. In fact, in many occupations, actual competence seems to take a backseat role anyway.

Confidence is an attribute that is very much in demand. As long as you keep calm and don't do anything stupid, other people view you as confident and probably even competent. I was also surprised that I had the reputation of being a womanizer, despite having had very little sexual experience back then. However, because I was not intimidated by the presence of women, that conclusion seemed unavoidable to some. Furthermore, if you manage to control your thoughts to some extent, which includes getting a hold on self-sabotaging thoughts, you will genuinely become more confident. This means that you will feel more confident.

In the end, mere outward appearances might be enough to make people believe that you have leadership abilities, even though not much has changed inside yourself. I do not want to make you believe that meditation is a way to bullshit yourself through life. Quite the opposite is true. Instead, the spillover effects of meditation may make people around you draw conclusions about you that are only partly justified. This allows you to enter a virtuous cycle of continuous self-improvement.

Social Interactions

With regards to your social interactions, meditation will have an almost immediate positive effect.

If you are deficient in that regard, your social skills could improve noticeably within weeks. This happens not because you learn to do something, but because you will get into the habit of stopping to do something unnecessary.

Maybe you get nervous around people, especially around attractive women. This is an aspect that is strongly exacerbated by a restless mind. Through meditation, you will learn to control your mind and your thoughts, which will help you in any social interaction. Insecure people tend to second-guess the actions of the people they deal with, even if there is no good reason to do so. Second-guessing easily leads to feeling nervous or being tense. This is reflected in your voice and gestures. Consequently, by not entertaining unnecessary thoughts and thus freeing up mental energy, you will be able to be more spontaneous. By reacting more intuitively, you may even be able to showcase more of your humor and wittiness.

Meditation is a pathway to becoming a lot calmer in general. That level of calmness will be your new baseline from which every interaction starts. Fumbling around and stuttering nervously may soon be much less of an issue than they are today. This could mean that the next time you see a cute girl in the library who smiles at you, you will not automatically lose your composure. Instead, you will find it not too difficult to return her smile or walk up to her, if you so desire. If the previous example sounded like something you could never do, it is due to psychological barriers. There is nothing that should stop you from interacting with strangers, especially if you find them attractive or interesting. However, by being unable to control your racing thoughts, you quickly get into a loop, resulting in you telling yourself that the girl could not possibly have been smiling at you, or that someone you are talking to does not like you but merely talks to you because he wants to be friendly.

Not all social interactions are pleasant. Surely, you have been in situations in which you wanted to stand up to someone or express a contrarian position in a discussion. In the end, you did not do so, despite knowing that you were right or that you could have influenced the discussion for the better. Too many experiences like that can make you harbor resentments or even turn you into a misanthrope. Learning to control your thoughts, instead of the other way round, will make you less nervous, help you present yourself better and more easily connect with people.

Examinations

Examinations are a big part of most of our life. This may be surprising to those of you who have yet to graduate from university. Depending on your chosen profession, there may be many more examinations left to pass before your career is fully established. This is particularly the case in accounting and finance. There are certifications to be earned in many other fields too, and some of those have high failure rates. That being said, university may be tougher, if only for the fact that your GPA (in the US) or overall degree classification (in the UK) determines whether you will even get a foot in the door in certain fields.

No matter how good a student you are, you may be afraid of examinations. This nervousness could be justified because you are poorly prepared and pin your hopes on the arguably implausible expectation that an upcoming exam will be a lot easier than previous exams you managed to get your hands on. Fear of failure due to being ill-prepared can be remedied. Just work harder! However, many students are well prepared and nonetheless fear failure. This is irrational because they should know that they will do well. Yet, despite having mastered the material to a reasonable degree, they are afraid of failing. Some even get caught in a cascade of negative thoughts: they will do poorly on the upcoming exam and on many others. Consequently, their GPA will tank and they will not land a good job. Finally, they conjure up a nightmarish scenario in which they end up living in the basement of the house of their aging parents, living off food stamps, and being a failure on every metric imaginable. Regardless of where you find yourself on this spectrum, you will arguably do a lot better if you get a hold on your thoughts.

In general, in an examination situation the effects of meditation yield enormous dividends. Not only will you be less disturbed by external events and be able to deal with intrusive thoughts, you will also, through repeated practice, be able to relax much more quickly. It is one thing to be able to relax when you are undisturbed while sitting in the lotus position, but it is quite another to do so when you are stressed out because of an upcoming exam. If you learn to do this, you can reasonably expect to do better with the same amount of work. Ideally, you will be able to maximize your potential because your thoughts no longer sabotage you.

Heated Arguments

A surprising amount of people have anger management issues, which is unfortunate as there is little to be gained by losing your composure. There are many situations that may justifiably make you angry, at least if you do not have a firm grip on your emotions. One of the most disgraceful displays of human behavior I experienced was when a Lufthansa flight out of Italy I was about to take was first delayed for ninety minutes, and later on canceled. Only a minority of the people in the queue waiting to speak to a service agent voiced their disapproval, but among those who did there were people who lacked all self-awareness. The worst was a middle-aged Italian guy in an expensive suit who wildly gesticulated while unleashing a torrent of expletives on the service staff. He only shut up after airport security showed up. That guy seemed oblivious that his inability to control his emotions wasted not only his time but also the service agent's time and the time of everyone who was still waiting for their turn.

I understand when people get upset when facing frustration. However, there is plenty of human behavior for which there is no excuse at all. Have you possibly dated someone who later turned out to barely be able to keep on top of things? People like that create chaos around them and it is only a matter of time until they, yet again, fall victim to their own inability of keeping themselves organized and making plans. A positive interpretation is that such people can learn to improve but there are also people who seem to be of inferior cognitive ability and simply cannot identify a weakness and systematically work on it. As a reader of this book, though, I presume you are smart, dedicated, and motivated enough to work on yourself.

There is a flip side to being able to control your

emotions: you will be able to stay calm when someone explodes in your face. Frankly, if you ever find yourself in such a situation, you should think long and hard about how you ended up in it because you probably ignored countless red flags. Concrete examples are histrionic girlfriends, emotionally immature colleagues, and abusive managers. Such people have in common that whenever something annoys them, they would rather unload their frustrations than address the underlying issue. You will find it a lot easier to not get caught up in that kind of emotional drama and walk away unharmed if you manage to cultivate a calm disposition.

Anxieties and Feelings of Insecurity

Less dramatic than clinically relevant aberrant psychological behavior are anxieties. Those can be crippling but I am more concerned with everyday occurrences. In the following, I largely focus on women as I have rarely encountered similar behavior in men. Women who are prone to suffering from anxieties, if not full-blown panic attacks, seem to follow a particular pattern. First, something innocuous happens, which leads to an association with an unwelcome memory. Instead of not dwelling on it and moving on, they unearth one negative association after another. It is worse if said negative emotion has led to an emotional breakdown in the past already. Before they know it, they are trapped in a circle of racing thoughts.

Consider how this played out with an emotionally unstable former girlfriend of mine. Sadly, she was unable to identify the emotional pattern she was trapped with. It roughly went as follows: she was unhappy about something, but instead of tackling the issue, she created conflict as a means of distraction. For instance, she may ask you to get some milk on the way to her place, and you forget it. You may think that the blame is on you, but you don't realize that even if you had gotten a carton of milk, something else would have upset her. She uses this as a justification for starting an argument. Clearly, you have now proven that you do not care about her. Seconds later, she is screaming at you. With such a person you cannot reason. To her, every single conclusion along the way is perfectly valid. I think the underlying issue is that such women do not have a firm grip on their emotions and quickly enter a circle of constantly reinforcing negative thoughts.

It may not be immediately obvious how the previous example relates to meditation. One of the biggest benefits of meditation is that it will teach you to not engage your mind in needless speculation. Let me spell out how this plays out for a novice, an intermediate practitioner, and someone very experienced. When novices have a random thought enter their mind, they tend to chase it. One thought leads to another, which may or may not be connected to the preceding thought they had. This is the essence of having a restless mind. An intermediate practitioner may still have many thoughts entering his mind but he will not engage them. Those thoughts just come and go. As a very experienced practitioner, however, you are used to meditating with an empty mind, which is an incredibly empowering experience. Thus, intrusive thoughts are not even an issue for you anymore.

Indeed, meditation should not be viewed in isolation of your daily life. The further you progress in your meditative practice, the more it will change how you react in everyday situations. Do you now see how this relates to people who do not have a firm grip on their emotions? In my view, emotionally unstable people have limited agency. Instead of themselves controlling their emotions, it is the other way round. One way of working on that problem is therefore to meditate in order to strengthen your mental stability.

The example of an old girlfriend of mine mentioned above was rather extreme, so let me present a milder variation that may be more relatable. Let's say you do something but the outcome is disappointing, so you question an entire series of future plans and ignore past successes. For instance, you may have built an ego around your mathematical ability, but then you find yourself in a class on abstract algebra. You spend an entire day on the worksheet, but you just cannot get anywhere. Does this mean that your possibly stellar previous academic record is for naught and that you should drop out or study something less challenging? Well, it depends. Negative feedback from your environment may be a legitimate reason to reevaluate your self-image. However, there is also pointless fretting over trivialities. With a clear head it is easier to decide what kind of situation you are facing. Are you genuinely on the wrong track in life or are you simply dealing with a temporary setback you should be able to overcome with perseverance? The latter should not lead to anxiety, while the former probably should. In any case, it is important that you keep moving forward.

Plenty of men end up in situations where their anxiety triggers a fight-or-flight response. They feel threatened and may say or do something they will soon afterwards regret. If this applies to you, then think about why you get aggressive. More often than not, it is a sign of insecurity. The subsequent question is: why are you insecure? Once you figure that out, you will be able to work on that part of your personality. Losing your temper and resorting to verbal abuse or even physical violence will hardly ever do you any good. You may think you have sound reasons to react as you do, but it is hardly more sensible than your girlfriend freaking out about some minor or possibly even imagined incident.

Meditation teaches you to keep a cool head. Ideally, you will learn to put your aggression and insecurities to work in a more beneficial way. After all, having a chip on your shoulder can be a powerful motivational force. This means that you won't show your extreme side in an argument. Meditation will also help you to avoid getting into such situations because occurrences that used to annoy or anger you, you will endure more easily. One day, you will rightly ask yourself why you even got mad about such incidents in the past.

Stress

I am probably the calmest person you will never meet. On the other hand, most people I encounter are of a more nervous disposition. I often observe this in my professional life. For instance, quite a few people have more on their plate than they can handle, at least from time to time. More often than not, the issue is not one of having too much to do *per se*. Instead, the problem is two-fold. First, many people cannot prioritize effectively. Second, they cannot focus properly. The first issue can be learnt fairly easily, the second not so much. However, meditation can increase your powers of concentration significantly. You may be surprised by how much you can get done, compared to others, if you simply focus on one task at a time and give it your undivided attention.

Being able to focus also leads to greater resilience against stress. You can surely think of situations in which stress negatively affected you. Yet, whether you experience something as stressful depends on your perception. Very few of us, if any, are ever in situations where our biological fight-or-flight response is appropriate. Instead, we push paper in the office, talk to colleagues, customers, or superiors. I have found that years upon years of meditation play a significant role in being able to remain calm even in situations in which many others likely would have lost their composure. This includes genuinely dangerous situations, such as when, while visiting a town in the South of Sweden, a Middle Eastern-looking man tried to rob me in broad daylight. I think I got out of this unharmed because he realized, after deflecting his attack calmly, that I would not be an easy mark.

Most stress I have been exposed to in my life came from unhinged women. I got out of such situations alive as well. Keeping my composure also kept me out of trouble with the law. To mention one particularly grave example: I once lived, thankfully only briefly, with a woman who fed off extreme emotions. This meant that she sometimes started fights over nothing. She could appear to be perfectly calm one moment and in the other Dr. Jekyll would turn into Ms. Hyde, meaning that she would explode in my face because she thought I was not paying any attention to her, never have, never will, and did not care about her anyway. Once she even threw a heavy jar at me. Had it hit me in the head in an unfortunate way, she could have killed me, and feminist judges would have of course not found any fault in her behavior. I saw it coming from the corner of my eye, so what amounted to attempted second-degree murder with a weapon did not come to fruition.

Upon realizing how utterly bonkers her behavior was, she apologized profusely. Long story short, I left her. I eventually learnt that she had a diagnosis of borderline personality disorder, but refused treatment. But why am I telling you this? Of course, she was an extreme case, but there are plenty of men out there who get into serious legal trouble because an emotionally unstable woman they were sexually involved with pushed them past their breaking point. Just imagine what an enraged guy could do to a woman in self-defense against an attack with a knife! If this does not sound crazy enough for you yet, then I should probably tell you that there are married women out there who provoke their husband into physically harming them in order to more easily get child custody and monetary compensation for the harm they indirectly inflicted on themselves by goading their husband into hitting them.

How do you think you would react in such a situation? If you think you would not be able to remain calm, then you may want to start devoting time to meditation. Your life could depend on you being able to react calmly in a dangerous situation.

Practice

Prerequisites

In this chapter, I discuss the prerequisites for meditation. There are not many, as you will see. It is more about what you do *not* need than what you need. First and foremost, you need a quiet place. Second, you may want to practice sitting in the lotus position for a more authentic experience. Third, you most certainly do not need to meditate in a group. Fourth, you definitely do not need to spend money on the bells and whistles that people in the New Age community hawk.

A Quiet Place

What you need more than anything else is a quiet place. As meditation is about confronting yourself with emptiness, any distraction is bad. Of course, you don't need to have a soundproof room or access to a bunker. All you need is enough space to sit down. I use a yoga mat for meditation, but you can as well just sit on a rug or even a towel.

I like to meditate in a room with white walls to look at, but that is not a necessity. After all, you can just close your eyes. Meditating with open eyes is more challenging. For that, you probably do not want to be in a room with garish wallpaper or paintings on the wall. While meditating with your eyes open is a greater challenge, there are no tangible rewards for it, so you are probably better off not bothering with it. Meditating with your eyes closed is, overall, preferable. You could say that this is a deeply democratizing aspect of meditation because it does not matter where you live, how young, tall, rich, and beautiful you are — with our eyes closed, the world looks just the same to all of us.

I will discuss it later on in detail, but let me already at this point mention that you do not need any additional equipment. Do not bother with candles, scented or not, incense sticks, or, what I consider an oxymoron, meditative music. Those are all pointless distractions that will do more harm than good. Again, a quiet room and something to sit down on is all you need. In fact, part of the beauty of meditation is that you do not need anything else to do it. It is advisable for a beginner to chose a quiet environment such as your bedroom. An advanced practitioner can easily reach a deep meditative state in a comparatively noisy environment as well. Very experienced practitioners are even able to sink into a deep meditative state quickly in almost any environment just by closing their eyes.

Revisiting the Lotus Position

Central to meditation as it is traditionally taught is the lotus position. It is easy to describe but not necessarily easy to sit in: sit down, put your left foot on your right knee, and then, while keeping the left foot on the right knee, put the right foot on the left knee. (You have seen an illustration earlier in this book, but I'm inserting it a second time below for your convenience.) You are welcome to swap the order by starting with putting your right foot on your left knee and so on. Please do not panic if you cannot sit in the lotus position. It is quite difficult to do so. Hardly anybody can do it right off the bat. There are alternatives, including some that you should be able to perform no matter how stiff you are. Even if you are among the more flexible among your peers, it may require significant practice to be able to sit in the lotus position, so please do not feel discouraged.

Figure 2: The Lotus Position

Some people are unable to sit in the lotus position due to their physiology. For instance, if you have very strong, muscular legs the lotus position is probably out of reach. Obese people may face the same problem. In the former case you probably want to keep your muscles, but in the latter you may want to consider shedding your excess weight, and not just because it will make it easier to meditate.

Rest your hands in your lap, one on top of the other, with your palms facing upwards. This is the traditional way of resting your hands. Alternatively, drop your arms in front of you, put one hand on top of the other, with your palms facing down. I find the latter more convenient and thus more natural than the traditional variant. Some gurus insist that you should put your hands on your knees, palms facing up, followed by the tip of the thumb and the tip of the index finger touching, forming a circle, and the remaining fingers stretched out. I consider this a highly artificial pose with no practical benefits whatsoever.

There are a few reasons why the lotus position is preferred among serious practitioners. The main reason is stability. You are firmly planted on the ground and you need to maintain some muscle tone to keep the position, which will keep you alert. A key aspect of the lotus position is keeping your spine straight. Personally, I view it as optional to keep your neck straight. In fact, when I meditate for a particularly long stretch of time I lower my chin.

There are also reasons often mentioned in support of the lotus position that are at best secondary. Let me go through them one by one. One, it is the most traditional way of meditating, therefore it presumably feels more serious to do so. Two, it adds an element of physical discomfort to meditation, further adding to any perceived seriousness. Three, there are clear practical benefits of the lotus position when meditating in a serious group. The third point largely applies to people who meditate in monasteries, as the monk assigned with watching over the group can more easily detect if you fall asleep and whack you on the shoulder with a paddle to jolt you out of that state.

The three secondary reasons I mentioned may not be very convincing to you. Quite frankly, you can meditate quite seriously without all that seriousness that is often peddled. The only convincing reason is stability, which makes the lotus position more comfortable than many other ways of sitting without support for your back. However, this is a moot point if you do not intend to meditate for long stretches of time. For a session lasting fifteen or thirty minutes, the lotus position is hardly required.

While I will discuss alternatives to the lotus position further down, I still think that people should experience dealing with both physical and psychological discomfort and learn to at least partly overcome both. The former is due to the lotus position itself, the latter is due to the realization that your mind may be very active when left to its own devices and bring up all kinds of unwelcome memories or negative thoughts, which you have not yet dealt with but instead normally suppress.

Let me encourage you to try sitting in the lotus position. You may find it easy to do so, but it is more likely that you won't. My suggested progress plan, which I outline later on, starts with very brief meditation sessions. Surely, you will be able to deal with minor physical discomfort for the duration of those sessions. Furthermore, you may be surprised how flexible you are if you push yourself a little bit. So, just try it! If you can, do it right now: First, put your left foot on your right thigh. If this worked well enough, bring your right foot to rest on your left thigh. If you are not flexible enough, this position may be difficult to maintain. This will make it difficult to meditate for a longer stretch of time, which is another reason why we will confine ourselves to very brief meditation sessions at first. Only after you can sit somewhat comfortable and without pain will we extend the duration of the sittings to five minutes.

It may be superfluous to mention, but let me state it anyway: if you feel pain or numbness at any point while meditating, then please stop immediately. Stretch or shake your legs for a little bit until you feel better. Slight discomfort is unproblematic. In fact, it is part of meditative practice to get used to such discomfort. Eventually, you should experience very little, if any, discomfort when meditating.

If the Lotus Position is too Demanding

Starting from the lotus position is of course ideal. However, if you do not exercise a lot, you may find it impossible to sit in it. The situation will be even worse if you are overweight. The remedy is to work on your body and change your eating habits, which will both have many more positive benefits.

It would be perfect if you managed to regularly attend a yoga class, preferably a dynamic one like Ashtanga yoga, as this will help you tremendously with improving your flexibility and building some strength, too.

Meanwhile, as you are busy losing weight and gaining strength with the exercise regime of your choice, a number of alternatives to the lotus position are available. None of those is ideal. They should only ever be considered an interim solution if you intend to meditate more seriously. Otherwise, pick whatever position is most comfortable for you. If you can't quite sit in the lotus position, then feel free to sit cross-legged. This position is a bit less stable. You will furthermore have a problem with the foot your other knee is resting on, as you will invariably get the feeling of pins and needles. Thus, your meditation sessions will probably not last as long as they otherwise could.

For some people, even sitting cross-legged on the floor is an issue. If this is the case with you, then you may seriously want to consider exercising more frequently. However, using a couple of cushions which you place underneath your buttocks (but not your legs), you may be able to sit cross-legged as well. This is a compromise, albeit not an especially good one as you may find it difficult to sit completely still. A better workaround is getting one or two yoga blocks, putting them on the floor with their largest side facing up and placing a thick blanket on top. This elevates your behind and provides sufficient support for the weight of your body. This way, keeping a balanced position will not be an issue, unlike when sitting on top of a stack of cushions.

If you have avoided doing any exercise for the last decade and prefer fast food over anything else, then you may be in the very unfortunate position that you have to resort to using a chair. If this applies to you, then please heed the warning because you are in a rather bad shape. Your lifestyle choices are slicing years off your life expectancy and negatively affect your well-being. In all honesty, if you have to sit in a chair to meditate, then I would recommend you get in shape first as this should be a much higher priority than learning how to meditate.

More on the Benefits of the Lotus Position

At first, the lotus position might be difficult to sit in. However, it has some benefits the various alternative positions do not provide. One of its benefits is that it is difficult to sit in that position. You can keep your balance in any other position too, but the lotus position requires greater effort, in particular compared to sitting on a chair with a backrest. Now you may wonder why that is supposed to be good. It's simply that sitting in a chair with back-rest does not require you to focus on your pose, which is one of the reasons why beginners are prone to let their thoughts drift off all too quickly. Thus, the lotus position can be a helpful crutch.

Again, meditation is supposed to feel uncomfortable at first. However, this is not supposed to appeal to your machismo or masochistic nature. The level of discomfort you feel will diminish over time, even if some slight discomfort may always be part of meditation for you. Eventually, you will learn to tolerate it, which is one way of measuring your progress. As a side note, monks in Zen temples meditate for many hours every day and in much greater discomfort than you will ever experience in the comfort of your living room, so do not even think of complaining.

Keeping your back straight is only one part of the lotus position. The other aspect, namely resting your feet on your thighs, has an important benefit as this prevents your feet from going numb. This probably will not happen if you meditate for half an hour or less.

Especially once you start pushing your limits, you will realize that the lotus position is unparalleled. Use a chair, and the backrest will become uncomfortable after a while; sit with your legs crossed, and notice that one of your feet will go numb due to the weight of the other leg that is resting on it.

In the lotus position, none of this will happen.

Meditation can be seen as a means of training both mind and body. You will learn to suppress your mind's tendency to drift off, which will eventually enable you to focus much better on any task. You will also learn to endure discomfort more easily, which may make you appreciate the comforts we enjoy in our pampered age. Thus, the discomfort you experience from sitting in the lotus position might pay unexpected dividends in your daily life.

Alternatives to the Lotus Position

For serious practitioners there is no alternative to the lotus position. No other position comes even remotely close. However, I want to expand further on some alternatives. These are sufficient for giving you some exposure to the benefits of meditation, but they will severely hamper your progress in the long run. That being said, most of you probably do not intend to meditate for hours, even after years of practice.

The best alternative to the lotus position is sitting cross-legged with a straight spine. If needed, use a pillow to support your buttocks. The main downside is that this position gets uncomfortable quickly, due to a feeling of numbness developing in the lower leg. A further downside is that the foot on which the thigh of your upper leg rests on puts you slightly off-center. For starting out, sitting cross-legged is viable, but more ambitious practitioners probably will want to move on to the lotus position as soon as possible.

If you cannot sit cross-legged, I suggest you lie down on your back. The benefit is that no matter how decrepit you are, you likely can lie down easily. However, the problem with lying down is that it is very easy to fall asleep. Thus, you should only meditate in that position while you are still fully awake.

It may happen that you find it very difficult not to fall asleep while lying on your back. In that case, get a stool. This will force you to keep your spine straight, which has the added benefit that it will keep you focused. Falling asleep while sitting like that should be difficult to achieve.

The worst position to meditate in is sitting on a chair with backrest or even an easy chair. Those may be more comfortable than a stool at the beginning, but that won't last long. On the other hand, an easy chair makes it very easy to drift off and fall asleep. Only resort to these options if there is a good reason why you cannot just lie down on the floor.

In all those alternative positions, place your hands in whatever way you find convenient and comfortable. If you sit cross-legged, I suggest you place

your hands the same way I recommend for the lotus position. In case you prefer any of the other
alternatives, just rest your hands on your thighs,
with your palms facing downwards.

Meditating in Groups

You now know what you need to know in order
to meditate: a quiet room and something to sit
on. Everything else is superfluous. Thus, let me
continue by discussing what you absolutely do not
need. First and foremost, you do not need other
people if you want to meditate. I have tried meditating in groups, over and over. What I have learnt
thus was that the average level of the practitioners
was relatively modest. I have even had encounters in which the person running the group session
was only able to sit cross-legged with some effort.
That was a Christian group that had adopted Zen
spiritualism into their practice and hoped to gain
new members that way. When I sat down in the
lotus position, the Christian Zen guru leading that
group, incidentally a priest in real life, looked at
me in utter disbelief. He experienced visible discomfort at the sight of having a newbie join who
seemed to have come much further than he had
during his alleged decade of experience in meditation and his forty years of adhering to the Christian
faith.

Other notable memories include an alleged master running a guided meditation workshop. He tried to discourage me from sitting in the lotus position as it was supposedly uncomfortable and couldn't possibly be good for me. Needless to say, in his group nobody, not even that guru himself, sat in the lotus position, and they did not even bother to try. In another group I briefly attended they followed some Indian guru. They were big on chanting mantras in a language they did not understand. I guess that was an example of different strokes for different folks. Of course, not all meditation groups are like that, but you better remind yourself that professional guidance does not necessarily imply professionalism.

I found it particularly bothersome that some meditation groups were hardly more than a pretense for people with an interest in spirituality to gather and get drunk together. Such was my impression when I attended a meeting at a Vajrayana Buddhism temple. I was quite taken aback when, after forty-five minutes of meditation, which included copious use of mantras, gongs, and incense, the master said, "And now let's all go downstairs and have some beers!" The rest of the evening was similar to what you can encounter in any students' bar, except that the people were a bit older and that the women presumably justified their promiscuity by believing that it improved their karma. In my opinion, such behavior completely contradicts the purpose of meditation, which is to reduce the amount of chaos in your life, not to add to it. If you want to socialize, get drunk, or get laid, then pursue those activities straight away. Meditating is by its very nature not a social activity. Especially after you have reached a deep meditative state, you will have neither the need nor the motivation to socialize afterwards because you will feel at peace with yourself and the world. It is incongruent to socialize right after meditating.

One particular aspect of group meditation will either prevent you from reaching mastery or make it much more difficult, namely the fact that group sessions are timed. In my experience, sessions lasted anywhere from fifteen to forty-five minutes. In rare cases, it may be a sixty-minute session, but in those, there is a strong tendency of the organizer to attempt spiritual indoctrination and tell you about how you are supposed to "open your chakras," "let your aura grow," or "open the third eye." You may also be pestered to donate money or buy overpriced worthless trinkets. After sampling every group I could find, I cherished meditating on my own in an undisturbed manner even more.

The issue with group meditation sessions is not only that the time may not be used effectively. The biggest problem is that you have to follow someone else's schedule. Maybe you don't feel like taking a thirty-minute ride during rush hour to reach the downtown Buddhist temple. You could just spend those thirty minutes meditating instead of driving. Furthermore, just like our education system hardly ever allows you to experience "flow" and continue doing something in the rare case you really enjoy it, so too do group sessions force you to stop meditating after a set amount of time. Like little Jimmy in elementary school who would like to draw for two more hours or spend additional time on trying to figure out a problem in mathematics but cannot do so because it is now time for a different subject, you too will be told that it is now time to move on. This may have a debilitating effect on your motivation.

You may now object that in Zen temples, as I wrote earlier, monks meditate in groups. However, in those settings, the role of the master is much different from what I have experienced in the West. Instead of focusing on a guru, those monks meditate on their own and just so happen to be sitting in the same room. The master walks around and whacks with a wooden plank any monk who is on the brink of falling asleep. Meditation as it is taught in the New Age industry could not be any more different from that.

Bells and Whistles

In addition to groups, there is something else you do not need: all those ludicrous bells and whistles that seem to be part and parcel of meditation in the West. That's all just based on people wanting to profit off the uncritical New Age herd. I'll briefly go through a few examples and elaborate on why you do not need them.

First, forget about meditative music or guided meditation. The latter is particularly bad as the narration of those recordings will prevent you from facing your own thoughts. The point of meditation is to give your mind the opportunity to confront you with largely unresolved issues, which will emerge as thoughts while meditating. If you listen to someone else's voice, this will be infinitely harder to achieve. Likewise, meditative music is at best a distraction, for the very same reason. It is less harmful than guided meditation, but that does not mean that there is any benefit to it.

Particularly among women have I noticed a preference for incense sticks and candles, especially scented ones. Unscented candles are a visual distraction, scented candles are also an olfactive distraction, and so are incense sticks. By the way, incense sticks are bad for your health, worse even than smoking cigarettes. No, meditation is not some kind of lifestyle, which is the preferred excuse of New Age acolytes for their frivolous spending. I view meditation as mental hygiene instead of a welcome pretense for buying useless clutter.

Next, there is the despicable tendency of meditation practitioners to buy trinkets such as Buddha statues or decorative pillows. There normally is no shortage of any kind of symbolism either. I think this is likewise just to appeal to women, which are overrepresented in New Age circles. Gongs might have a practical use to signify the end of a meditative session, but this is only a ceremonial gesture and completely superfluous. You may argue that a gong is needed for authenticity, but then you may want to recall the title of this book. If you meditate on your own, a regular alarm will do or — I know, it is a revolutionary concept! — you just meditate for however long you feel like meditating.

Lastly, some schools advocate the use of mantras. It would be less ridiculous if they were in a language those people are actually able to understand. Instead, they repeat a few phrases or just syllables. Again, it is a pointless distraction. Just try it out yourself after you have gotten some practice with meditation! You will find that hearing a mantra, let alone chanting one yourself, severely distracts from the main goal of meditation. You will be able to mentally relax much better without them.

Meditation Stripped-Down

While I have been following a more traditional approach to meditation, built around mastering sitting in the lotus position, I have to bluntly state that it is not necessary to do so for a more casual, yet still reasonably effective meditative practice. Good luck finding anyone in the New Age industry making a similar statement, though. Based on my over two decades of experience, the value of meditating in the lotus position is largely due to it being part of a ritual. However, you can do perfectly well without it, and even without the experience of overcoming physical discomfort in meditation. Some of you may find some value in overcoming physical limitations, which is why I do not want to denounce the lotus position as bullshit. Of course, there is the obvious advantage of stability, which enables you to meditate for very long stretches of time. Very few of you are going to go down that particular path, though.

I have, for a long time, bought into a ritualistic approach to meditation myself. While there is comfort in following rituals — you probably have integrated several routines as part of your life, which are rituals in all but name — it is not the case that sitting in the lotus position needs to be part of an effective meditation ritual. I would say that if you are curious, try sitting in the lotus position, but also consider the alternatives I mentioned earlier. Those will be good enough to let you reap a large part of the benefits of meditation. It took me a bit of time to admit this myself. This was largely due to having meditated in the lotus position for so many years. Of course, the more ingrained your habits are, the less willing you may be to change them.

The easiest alternative to the lotus position is lying down on your back, as it is arguably the most comfortable position your body can be in. After all, you lie down to sleep, instead of sitting in an easy chair or intertwining your legs in order to sit in the lotus position. However, you should not lie down in your bed as that might interrupt your circadian rhythm. It is poor sleep hygiene to do anything else in your bed besides sleeping and having wild sex. For lying down, a carpet is a good start. No, you do not have to buy one. If you have a thick carpet in your living room, you are set. A yoga mat is likewise suitable.

While sitting down in a comfortable easy chair or lying down on the ground, you can just as well focus on the core of meditation, as outlined in this book: focusing on your breathing, if you need that crutch, trying to clear your mind, and learning to be alone with your thoughts. It is perfectly fine if this sounded cryptic as I will discuss the details later on.

You may want to interject that meditation groups that do not insist on the lotus position and, for instance, let you sit cross-legged could have the same motivation. This is decidedly wrong as they still buy into the belief that you need to sit in a particular way. They cannot sit in the lotus position, so they give you some kind of ersatz version of it, which is uncomfortable to sit in for a long time. Just like ersatz coffee is worse than the real thing, sitting cross-legged is worse than sitting in the lotus position. Their implication is that it would be more beneficial to sit in the lotus position, but since they cannot do that, due to lacking the willpower to continuously work on that skill, they tell you that there is an alternative that is essentially as good.

Probably quite a few people develop their own meditative practice over the years, which may be quite similar to what I outline in this chapter. On that note, I recall a routine my late grandmother had. She just rested in an easy chair in her living room, not doing anything, not reading the newspaper, not listening to the radio nor watching TV. She just sat there, with her hands resting in her lap. Normally, one of her cats would at one point hop into her lap. I know about that because I grew up in saner times in which people did not lock their front door when they were home, so I ended up barging in on her a few times when I was a kid.

The main relevance of the lotus position is during long meditation sessions. It genuinely starts to make sense once you are able to meditate for an hour straight. Yet, it may not make a lot of sense to devote that much time to meditation. The lotus position forces you to sit upright and if you get tired, your upper body will start to move involuntarily. Your swaying would be the cue for the monk watching the group to hit you on the shoulder with a wooden paddle to prevent you from falling asleep. I think that it is impossible to sleep while sitting in the lotus position because you need to keep your back straight. Thus, it will be obvious if you are getting sleepy. Yet, all of that is of dubious value as you most likely are not interested in meditating in a Zen monastery.

Lastly, let me remark that there are good reasons why meditation gurus, even if they have realized that they bought into bullshit, will never tell you any of this. It simply boils down to money and status. As absurd as it may sound, you can be a guru even if you cannot sit in the lotus position, which is about as plausible as virgins teaching other guys how to get laid. For the gullible New Age herd, ambience is very important, though. That crowd vastly prefers appearance over substance. How do you think such people would react if there was a guru who just handed out blankets and told people to lie down and clear their mind? It would be downright ludicrous to them. A lot of the ritualism surrounding commercial or sect-style meditation is indeed built on bullshit, but people who buy into it want precisely that.

Particular flavors of bullshit serve as unique selling propositions, targeting different crowds. People in that market do not want to hear that they could achieve the same or better results for free at home, or worse, that all they need is a quiet place. Instead, they desire the souped-up experience because they want to be part of something bigger. This is particularly ironic as those people normally do not want to pursue meditation more seriously anyway and could get better results if they just spent some time meditating on their own at home.

Getting Started

By now you should be itching to get started with meditation. We will aim for a very modest goal at first, namely meditating for two minutes. This might sound quite short, and it is. If you are used to looking for ways to distract yourself, then even a two-minute session can prove surprisingly difficult to endure. Yet, in such a short amount of time, all important aspects of meditation will be encountered. You will have to find a (hopefully) comfortable position for your body, block distractions, and confront a likely restless mind. I will say more about breathing in the next chapter. For now, just breathe as you normally do.

Facing Your Restless Mind

Through meditation you will encounter two kinds of discomfort, physical and psychological discomfort. The former is due to sitting in the lotus position, which may take some time getting used to. However, as I have discussed earlier, there are alternatives to the lotus position which spare you physical discomfort, but at some cost. The latter, psychological discomfort, is a more severe issue. It results from being confronted with emptiness. The question is what your mind will latch on to when left to its own devices, while your books, smartphone, laptop, or video game console are out of reach. Of course, you could avoid all of that by listening to meditative music in order to give your mind something else to focus on, but doing so would completely bereave you of the benefits of meditation. Your mind will not overcome any obstacles by listening to chants, instrumental music, or ambient sounds.

The biggest surprise for most people is that as soon as they sit down in a quiet environment without any external stimuli, they have many thoughts popping up in their mind, often disconnected ones. In the scriptures of gurus and classical works in the area of Eastern philosophy, this is often interpreted as a sign of unresolved issues. Indeed, you may remember someone who wronged you or decisions you regret having made. There may have been opportunities you regret not having taken. Your thoughts may also be oriented towards the present or future. Some focus more on unresolved current issues, others on problems you expect having to deal with in the future. It can take a long time to let go of those thoughts. Hopefully, your thoughts are not all gloomy. Yet, the same principle applies in the opposite case as well. If happy thoughts enter your mind, you should likewise not hold on to them, as pleasant as they may be.

Based on my experience teaching people meditation and based on my own progress, it seems to be the case that negative thoughts are much more prevalent than positive ones. This makes perfect sense, as your mind is pointing you towards unresolved issues. However, a lot of people worry far too much. They let themselves get bogged down by past misfortunes and worry excessively about potential future disasters. In more tragic cases, they are so obsessed with their past and future that they forget to properly deal with the problems they face in the present. A much more sensible approach is to mine past unpleasant experiences for valuable lessons and deal with present problems to the best of your ability, which will likely already prepare you well for the future. In that regard, meditation is a viable method for learning to focus on what is important.

What holds many people back are vague concerns about future events. Most often, they consist of nothing but baseless conjecture. They worry about things they should not even worry about because the eventual outcome will be much different anyway. Therefore, there is no point in dreaming up horror scenarios about you missing your flight, fumbling up an important business meeting, getting hit by a truck, or anything like that. It amounts only to fruitless expenditure of mental energy. Meditation is one way of getting a hold of that.

In general, you can expect your mind to become much calmer over time through meditation as you learn to not get distracted by entertaining unproductive thoughts. This is the key part of meditation. That kind of mental progress can aptly be described as strengthening of your will. You learn to control your thoughts and you learn to focus as well as to relax. Every little bit of progress in that regard is commendable, considering that many people cannot even sit still. You will learn to not only do that but also to control your mind and perceive reality more clearly.

Making Meditation More Accessible

In order to lower your resistance to meditation, I suggest starting with two-minute sessions. Even slightly longer sessions of five minutes or so may prove uncomfortably long for a beginner. Indeed, when starting out, it may be difficult to sit down for more than a few minutes as you will quickly feel discomfort. Probably you will want to reflexively pick up your smartphone. Given that we are in an age where people have been collectively working towards having the attention span of goldfish, I recommend taking baby-steps at first, and I mean it. The prospect of meditating for fifteen minutes may not sound like much when you read about it, but just try it, and you will notice that it is a lot harder than you might think. To minimize frustration, we will therefore start with two-minute sessions, because even that will feel a lot longer than it is.

Before you start, please set an alarm clock. This is necessary because you will find it very difficult to judge the amount of time that has passed. It will also hopefully prevent you from entering a thought-loop that circles around the questions of how much time has passed already or how much time is left. Setting the alarm should make you certain that this issue has been taken care of, allowing you to fully focus on meditation.

I advise you to stick to two-minute meditation sessions for at least one week. Pushing yourself too hard too soon is a recipe for failure, and we do not want you to feel burnt out from meditating for half an hour or more just because you wanted to prove to yourself that you can meditate for that long. The discomfort of such a long meditation session would likely be very unpleasant for you and make you not want to pursue meditation fur-

65

ther.

Another benefit of sticking to two minutes at first is that you cannot possibly have a rational reason not to do it. I don't care how busy you claim your life is — you surely can spare *two minutes* out of twenty-four hours. You may even fit two short sessions into your busy day, one after getting get up and another one before going to bed.

Apart from the minor discomfort due to having to sit still for two minutes, which surely feels like torture to some people, the much bigger challenge is controlling your thoughts. You will notice that it is not that easy to just sit down and not think of anything. All kinds of thoughts, often unresolved issues, will crop up. If you are more pragmatic, you may even wonder when the alarm you set is eventually going to go off. After all, if you do not do anything besides sitting on the floor, perceived time can pass very slowly, turning two minutes into a seemingly much longer period of time. In any case, you should not feel surprised if you already felt a bit calmer after meditating for just two minutes.

Try it!

Armed with the information you have received so far, I want you to put this book down and meditate for two minutes. Now! If that is not possible, for instance, because you sit on the bus or train or because your manager should believe that you are working, then please do so at a time that is more suitable for you and do not read on. Otherwise, find a quiet place, set a timer, and go ahead. Sit down and close your eyes. Just try it, even if you think you are not ready yet and should read more about meditation. It will neither be as difficult nor as easy as you expect it to be. Please do not continue reading this book before having done so, as we are going to look at some of your experiences.

Turn this page over when you are ready.

You have now meditated for two minutes, or you have disregarded my advice. If it is the latter, then I would like to let you know that you would get a lot more out of the current section of this book if you had meditated. From now on I assume that you did indeed just meditate for two minutes.

So, how do you feel now? Probably you feel refreshed. I am more interested in how you experienced your brief meditation session, though. Most likely, as soon as you closed your eyes, mental images popped up. Maybe you remembered something someone said or something you should do. In any case, it is likely that random thoughts entered your mind. People do not often seem to encounter abstract thoughts during their meditations. Sure, you may get inspiration for a report or presentation you have been working on or some other problem that occupies your mind most of the day, but that is rather the exception than the rule. Instead, people much more often encounter thoughts about the present, past, or future. Those are often trivial thoughts, too.

An example of a thought regarding the present can be as banal as remembering that you have to buy soap because you are about to run out of it. This is just a silly example. It does not matter what kind of thought enters your mind. Just try to let it go. The last thing you want to do is to hold on to a particular thought so that you can make a note once the timer has gone off. You may also feel the urge to engage your thoughts further. For instance, if it occurred to you that you really need to get some soap, the next obvious step may be to go through all the items in your household, think of which ones need to be replenished and mentally create a shopping list while meditating. Well, why don't you just visualize the trip to the supermarket or convenience store right afterwards? This is obviously an exaggeration. The point is that eventually you will have to stop engaging your thoughts. You are better off doing so right away.

More meaningful might be memories of past experiences. This may include happy memories but you could also get confronted with memories of traumatic experiences. Consequently, it is not always pleasant to meditate. Yet, you will learn to face your demons and you will personally grow as a consequence. I will later on discuss in more detail how to deal with such thoughts. It is not based on blocking them, but by resolving the issues that cause them. Meditation may even put your psychoanalyst out of his job.

Lastly, there is the issue of uncertain future events. But since neither you nor me nor anybody else seems to have a working crystal ball, thinking excessively about the future is, for the very most part, unproductive. This may refer to pleasant as well as unpleasant situations. Maybe you want to ask your boss for a raise, but never dare to. Someday you hopefully will, but now it has been six months already and the time has never been right. Or you want to ask a cute girl out on a date and you know if you do not act soon, somebody else invariably will. Maybe you have a tendency to plan everything ahead and you subconsciously know that you cannot consider all eventualities. This is something people have to learn to accept.

In general, random thoughts tend to be an expression of an unorganized life. This is especially true if those random thoughts do not disappear as you gain more practice with meditation. I will later on discuss what I call mental hygiene, which entails keeping your mind uncluttered. Most of those tips take little time or effort to implement, but will improve your life dramatically.

Meditation and Sleep Deprivation

Meditating for even just two minutes can teach you a lot about yourself. I have already discussed symptoms of a restless mind, but there is also feedback from your body. I have frequently witnessed that people who are under a lot of stress and lack rest sometimes fall asleep during even a very brief meditation session. You should not be too surprised if that happens to you. However, if your

70

alarm clock woke you up at the end of what was supposed to be a meditation session, then your body gave you an important warning sign. It is quite obvious that you should grant yourself more time to rest and recover. The last thing you should skimp on is the quality and quantity of your sleep.

Contrary to what some people believe, the time you spend sleeping is not wasted. In an ideal world you would not even need an alarm clock, but instead go to bed when you feel tired and get up only after you have naturally woken up. There cannot be enough sleep, unlike some people claim. I refer to actual sleep, not time idled away lying in bed after waking up. There are outlandish but allegedly scientific claims according to which you shorten your expected lifespan if you sleep too much. The studies I read on that topic all seemed to be deficient in one way or another. I would not be surprised, as it is the case in many other fields of science, if industry-funded research was to blame for such results. Do not call me a conspiracy theorist, but just consider this possibility: If it turned out that people needed more than eight hours of sleep to fully recover, don't you think that labor unions or possibly even human rights organizations would put pressure on politicians to reduce working hours?

Not many people have the freedom to go to bed and rise whenever they feel like. Yet, with some discipline you should be able to get enough sleep every day. If this means that you need to cut down on some of your hobbies or the time you spend consuming media, then so be it. As long as you have a hard time not falling asleep when meditating, you have a deficiency in that regard. If you took care of that problem, then it would not only be easier for you to properly meditate — this is the least of the benefits of getting proper rest — you would also greatly improve your quality of life.

Getting Started for Real

Starting With Meditation

Meditating for two minutes is just to get you started. Your goal should be to meditate once or twice a day. Make it a habit, not unlike brushing your teeth! First, you need to get used to meditating for two minutes. This should not take you more than about a week or two. Afterwards, increase the duration of your meditation sessions to a longer interval. I recommend five minutes. The mid- to long-term goal is to further increase the time interval, first to ten and afterwards to fifteen minutes.

Once you are able to comfortably meditate for fifteen minutes, you will likely hit a sweet spot, meaning that the amount of time you invest and the benefits you reap are in a highly favorable relation to each other. Just like with everything else in life, there are diminishing returns, and they kick in quickly. While gurus may make vague claims about the endless depths of meditation and blather on about all the insights that await you, if you only followed their school and transferred a fraction of your income to their bank account every month, the reality is that there is a limit to how much you arguably would want to relax anyway. Relaxation and mental clarity are both a means to an end, after all. On the other hand, meditating for hours a day is an end all by itself, and one of dubious value. Instead, set a limit and stick to it.

For at least half a year, I recommend meditating with a timer. Ideally, there are little or no distractions around when you meditate. This means that you will find it next to impossible to gauge how much time has passed. A similar phenomenon occurs after you turn off the light and want to fall asleep but can't. In such a situation, it is equally difficult to accurately guess how much time has passed. It may be a lot less than you think, but you could just as well underestimate how much time has passed. With meditation, taking a break and checking the time is highly counterproductive, so you will be much better off delegating timekeeping to an alarm clock.

A timer is also necessary to help you build discipline. Especially as you learn to reach deeper meditative states, you can easily lose track of time, which can go both ways. Just as you probably do not want to get up after five minutes, which may feel like half an hour, so you similarly also do not want to lose yourself in meditation. There is very little risk of that happening when you are starting out, but once you are able to sit in the lotus position comfortably, you may end up spending an hour or more meditating, even if you did not intend to do so. For that reason, I still use a timer, even after more than two decades of meditation.

Being in a prolonged deep meditative state will easily make you lose track of time. Experiencing this once or twice is a worthwhile experience, even if only for the insight that there are diminishing returns in meditation. Those diminishing returns may very well be due to external constraints as you have something else to do than accidentally meditating for hours. I am not saying that you should not explore meditation. However, the focus of *Meditation Without Bullshit* is on integrating meditation into your daily life instead of making it the center of it.

Speaking of the duration of meditation sessions, you will probably realize after a few months that a regimen that consists of no more than a daily five or ten-minute session is sufficient to reach a level of mental clarity you once thought impossible to achieve. Later on, I will discuss meditative states, and one aspect is that the more experienced you are, the quicker you reach a certain meditative state. This means that an advanced practitioner reaches a deeper state after one minute than a novice would after even one hour, if he could only sit for that long.

Breathing

Many people breathe in a shallow manner. Their short breaths increase their heartbeat and possibly even make them anxious. Then again, I might be mixing up cause and effect. Yet, for meditation you have to breathe deeply. Once you have gotten used to breathing that way, you might want to make it your default way of breathing. Long deep breaths have a calming effect all by itself, which you will notice once you deliberately breathe this way in your daily life. As opposed to shallow, short breaths, long, deep breaths supply you with more oxygen. I think it is a more natural way of breathing.

This may have sounded somewhat abstract. In short, shallow breathing means that you draw air into your chest. If you do not breathe this way, try it out for a little bit. To me, it feels quite uncomfortable. It is almost anxiety-inducing. Deep breathing, on the other hand, makes use of your diaphragm. To practice it, either sit down on a chair without using the backrest or stand up and put your hands on your ribcage. Then breathe deeply with your diaphragm instead of into your chest. Shallow breathing lifts your chest, while diaphragmatic breathing expands your midriff. This probably looks less impressive on the beach when you are about to hit on the ladies, but it is a more wholesome way of breathing.

After breathing out, there is a short pause, which happens naturally. Take another breath when your body triggers it and do not interfere with the breathing cycle too much. The goal is to let it happen. I suggest that you try to adopt this as your standard method of breathing. It might take you a few days if you are not used to engaging your diaphragm while breathing as it takes time to change a habit. After about one week you should have become accustomed to it.

One aspect that is sometimes stressed is to focus on your breathing while meditating. I view this as a crutch. People focus on their breathing because they do not want to experience the restlessness of their mind. By doing so, they cheat themselves out of many of the positive aspects of meditation. If you find it difficult to make it through a few minutes of meditation, then focusing on your breathing may be excusable. However, you should stop doing so sooner rather than later as it will only impede your progress. Focusing on your breathing can be a helpful crutch when starting out. I will discuss this issue in more detail further below.

Meditation and Your Daily Life

I find it irritating how meditation is normally marketed in the West. Often, the focus is on a full-time professional guru who is presented as an ideal worthy of emulation. Of course, you, the target of such marketing, are likely not active in the guru business yourself. You cannot sit back and enjoy life without any perturbations. Part of modern life in the West, for better or worse, consists of juggling many responsibilities, such as your job, relationship, children, and hobbies. If you cut out all of that, you are not left with a lot. Fake gurus are aware of that, too. In the extreme, they sell their disciples New Age doctrines, but privately maintain a fleet of Rolls-Royce limousines and a small army of mistresses.

Meditation is a great tool for relaxation. Yet, it is not a panacea. No matter what you do, you will not be able to eliminate all sources of stress and uncertainty from your life, simply because, as the trite saying goes, no man is an island. There is too much that is out of your control. In this context, I would like to briefly address two common misguided beliefs, which are frequently exploited by shady businessmen. First, as much as you may think your job constrains you and keeps you from reaching your goals, whatever they may be, working for yourself is by no means a solution to that problem. Building a business that runs itself is no small feat, and if it was that easy to do, competition would spring up quickly and go after your piece of the pie. Also, you are likely to work a lot harder than you would sitting in your comfortable office chair. Of course, I am painting with very broad strokes, but if you wanted an easy ride, you are a lot better off putting in your time at work in exchange for a steady paycheck. Second, there is the financial independence crock that has been making the rounds. At the time of writing, we have had many years of zero-interest rate policies. Yet, the financial independence crowd is unperturbed. A consequence of zero-interest rate policies, though, is that stable returns are nowadays very difficult to achieve. There are asset bubbles everywhere you look, yet people think the party will just keep going. It will, but only until the next bubble bursts.

Realistically, you are stuck on the same treadmill as most everyone else. Yet, meditation can help you lead a more fulfilled life. Sure, reevaluate some of your goals, particularly if your health is suffering. If you bought this book because you wanted to squeeze more productivity out of your day, then the answer is that you need to get rid of some of your responsibilities because if you do not get enough rest, do not allow yourself some time to recharge, and neglect your health, then thinking that a few minutes of meditation will do the trick would be severely misguided.

One Thought Begets Another

It is much easier said than done that all you have to do to progress with meditation is not engage your thoughts. Just let go of them! Once you have mastered this skill, it will indeed be easy, but it can take some effort, just like any other skill. Eventually, it will seem natural and effortless and you will wonder what the problem was.

At first, pay attention to how your thoughts drift off. You have a random thought, which you use as the basis for making a conjecture. This is an active process. It may take a lot of time and practice to acquire a relatively undisturbed mind because random thoughts will simply keep popping up over and over. Yet, engaging them is something you actively do and which you should stop early on. You are not even sure whether A is going to happen, so why do you worry about B and C? This is also a great piece of advice for living your life as it will make you calmer and more relaxed in general. Meditation is a way of practicing this habit, and it will spill over into your daily life quickly. It should take you just about a month or so of constant meditative practice until you start noticing a difference. Even if you may not notice a difference, your close friends probably will. The other way people start to drift off is akin to day-dreaming. You grasp a thought or a memory and elaborate on it. It is not as bad as making baseless conjectures about future events, but quite similar in nature nonetheless.

Slowly learning to control your thoughts this way is just one part of the equation. In addition, it is necessary to learn to endure calmness and not try to look for something to think about for the purpose of keeping your mind occupied. Latin has the expression *horror vacui*, which translates to "being afraid of emptiness." This describes many people's nervousness that results from not having anything to do as the emptiness they have to deal with reveals whether they enjoy their own company. An expression of this phenomenon is social media addiction. Media consumption in general, if it only has the goal of keeping your time occupied, is problematic. Making use of any kind of entertainment is surely more pleasing than sitting in front of a blank piece of paper and realizing that you have nothing to write about and that you are a dreadfully boring person.

Learning those techniques takes time. However, it is a gradual process. Over time you will reap more and more of the benefits. This should also be motivation enough to keep going. Once you reach a stage where you no longer engage most of the thoughts that appear in your mind, you have come a long way. Right now, you are at the very beginning of that journey.

How to Let Go of Your Thoughts

It may sound flippant if I tell you to just let go of your thoughts. A friend of mine remarked that it is similar to telling an alcoholic, "Just stop drinking!" It is not that easy. Instead, it takes significant practice as it amounts to nothing less than changing what may very well be a lifelong and heavily ingrained habit, namely engaging unproductive thoughts. One clear marker of mastery in meditation is that you are able to sit down to meditate, with a completely clear head, and are able to meditate for however long you want, without even having any thoughts come up at all. It is a sign of even greater mastery if you are able to clear your mind at will during the day, no matter what you may be doing or what emotional state you may be in.

Mastery is the endpoint. But how do we get there? Well, let me dampen your enthusiasm by stating that it may take you many years. Without serious practice you will never even get close to it. As a crutch, you may start by focusing on your breathing. You breathe in and pay attention to not only the sound of breathing in and out but also to movements of your body, such as the expansion of your diaphragm. Focus on the sensation of inhaling, preferably through the nose, as well. Then you focus on the brief pause that naturally happens before exhaling. Exhaling follows the same principle. You pay attention to the sound the air creates as it is moving through your body. Pay attention to how your diaphragm contracts and how the air passes through your nostrils.

By focusing on your breathing, you give your mind something to focus on. Paying close attention to your body while breathing will therefore make it a lot more difficult for your mind to come up with an assortment of random thoughts. Unfortunately, focusing on your breathing is a distraction. It is worse than a crutch. You don't attack the problem of letting go of your thoughts. Instead, you give your mind something to do, which keeps it from coming up with random thoughts. Focusing on your breathing is merely an attempt to keep your mind occupied, and this keeps you from facing the genuine challenge of meditation: facing your own mind.

There is a particular danger as well: focusing on

your breathing is at best a very shallow first stage of proper meditative practice. Yet, you will find people who have spent years meditating and who have the misguided belief that meditation *means* sitting in the lotus position and focusing on your breathing. This is so wrong it's not even funny. Frankly, it is a downright absurd statement. It is even more absurd than, for instance, claiming that doing mathematics means sharpening your pencil and pulling out a white piece of paper. You arguably need pencil and paper for that purpose. Yet, focusing on your breathing is not a prerequisite for meditating, not in the least.

What focusing on your breathing might teach you is that you can sit still without having a myriad of thoughts enter your mind. However, the reason for that is not that you have learnt to control your mind but that you keep your mind busy by observing your breathing. I don't want to claim that this cannot have a calming effect. Yet, at one point you will have to take the crutches off. You will have to learn to meditate without focusing on your breathing and instead observe your mind. At this point your real journey begins. This leads to the question of what to do when some random thought enters your mind. In the beginning, too many thoughts might enter your mind for you to focus on any particular one. If you are stuck in that phase, it can be helpful to hold on to one of those thoughts. Feel free to even actively engage it, until you get to the point where the number of thoughts entering your mind becomes more manageable. Depending on how hectic your life is, this may take you a while. It could be weeks or even many months. During that time, your experience with meditation may amount to observing how your mind gets slightly less chaotic in the course of ten to fifteen minutes, which is certainly a good start.

After some time practicing meditation you should have reached a point where thoughts will only occasionally enter your mind. Whenever this happens, you actively engage this thought. It is irrelevant what it is. Let's say it is a happy memory. In that case, you end up daydreaming. Instead of doing that, try to merely fixate the thought. Focus on that happy memory but do not actively engage it. View it like a picture. Then drop it. You can do this with any kind of thought that enters your mind while meditating. Instead of actively engaging it, you merely observe it. Negative thoughts can be dealt with the same way. In my case, I used to suppress certain negative memories. Through meditation, I got confronted with them again. Repeated exposure allowed me to deal with them and make my peace, meaning that certain negative memories stopped having any power over me. They no longer upset me. I could simply observe those memories dispassionately and eventually move on. Once you have gotten to the point where you can observe thoughts instead of engaging them, start dropping them faster. You will notice that by that point, random thoughts should enter your mind at irregular intervals, but certainly much less often than when you started out with meditation.

I just introduced the concept of *dropping* a thought. This is hopefully a more intuitive metaphor than telling you to let go of your thoughts. Yet, those two verbs mean the exact same thing in this context. As you progress further, you should be able to very quickly let go of any thought that enters your mind while meditating. In my case, it is exceedingly rare that this happens, and if it does, that thought disappears as quickly as it emerged, letting me enjoy the calmness of my mind. With continuing practice, random thoughts should enter your mind more and more rarely, not just when meditating but in everyday life as well.

Proper Meditation

I have covered all important theoretical aspects of meditation. Now it is time for everything to come together. It is time for your first real practical session. Make sure you will not get disturbed, which means that you should turn off the TV, radio, computer, and phone. If you are not living alone, close the door and make sure nobody will barge into the room. Hopefully, you are able to sit in the lotus position. If not, then pick one of the alternatives I described earlier.

The next question is whether to close your eyes or keep them open and stare at the wall. It is great if there is a blank wall in front of you or just some even-colored surface, maybe the door, to which you can position yourself so that it fills your whole field of view. Any gadgets, furniture, clothes, books or whatever else you see lying around will only distract you and make it harder for you to meditate and get a hold of your thoughts. If you are sitting still and have nothing that occupies you, your mind may be quick to find something to latch on to and suddenly you think you have to call one of your friends to chit-chat. If you have the impression that the room you are in would be too distracting, then either find a different spot — or simply meditate with your eyes closed. For added difficulty, meditate with open eyes. This allows you to experience your mind's tendency to distract itself much more strongly. Thus, you will arguably make faster progress compared to meditating with your eyes closed. When you are just starting out, it can be easier to close your eyes, so if you find it too difficult to sit still with your eyes open, then just close them.

Another aspect that often comes up is the time of

day. Personally, I prefer to meditate before going to bed because it allows me to relax and subsequently fall asleep with ease. Others meditate in the morning because they think it wakes them up properly. To some extent, it is a matter of personal taste, and of course there is nothing wrong with making meditation part of both your morning and evening routine.

You have found a spot. Now set the timer and sit down in the lotus position. Afterwards, breathe in, and breathe out, deeply. It may help you to focus on your breathing, but, as I wrote earlier, this is a crutch you will eventually have to let go of. Keep going until your timer rings. While meditating, do not try to engage any thoughts that come up. That is all there is to it. The goal is to reach and maintain mental clarity. Make meditation a ritual with a fixed number of steps you always perform. Ideally, sit in the same spot at the same time every day. Make it a habit.

Progressing

Meditating for two minutes is just so that you get started. After a few days, I want you to increase the time span to five minutes per session, no matter if it's once or twice a day. It is important to make it a habit. Otherwise it is too easy to say to yourself that you are tired or have better things to do with your time. Once you have gotten comfortable with five minutes, you can gradually increase the interval. My progression was from 5 to 15 minutes. I eventually increased the time in 15-minute steps until I could sit for an hour. This was partly due to my desire to see how far I could push myself or how deep a meditative state I could reach. I eventually went well beyond that, but that is hardly necessary.

Interestingly, the more practice you get, the less time you need to spend meditating for the same effect. In the next chapter I will describe meditative states. At first, it can take a long time to just reach the second one, but with regular practice, you may go through the first two states within seconds and be able to reach a deeper and more relaxing meditative state after five minutes than you would have reached after forty-five minutes one year earlier.

Also, let me reiterate that I strongly recommend that you use a timer because you won't be able to judge for how long you have been meditating. At first, you may think you have been meditating for twenty minutes, even though it were less than five because you are not used to it. Later on, you may think you had only meditated for ten minutes when in fact it was closer to an hour. This is because in a state of relaxation with no external stimuli, there is no way to keep track of time.

Once you have reached a state of being able to meditate for half an hour with ease and reach a deep meditative state, you will notice that the calmness carries over to your daily life and affects your personality in a positive way. This is when you will start to experience the benefits I have described at the beginning of the book to a much more significant degree. It is the beginning of mastery.

Meditative States

While meditating, you will encounter a number of meditative states. The first is *chaos*, which refers to the restlessness of your untamed mind. Chaos eventually gives way to *clarity*, which describes your empty mind while meditating. If you can reach that state, or even if you only manage to catch a glimpse of it every now and again, you will be able to reap quite a bit of what meditation has to offer. Indeed, clarity is the state you should work towards achieving. It is within reach for all of you.

There are further meditative states to discover. I mention them in this book mainly because I do not intend to write another book on meditation. Even the first one of those further stages, *warmth*, will only be reached by a fraction of you. Subsequent states will be elusive for all but an extremely small number of you. You are therefore arguably better off viewing those parts as entertainment.

Chaos and Clarity

When you start out, you will first encounter a state of manifold, confusing thoughts. It will be difficult to keep your head clear for even a few seconds because you are not used to not occupying your mind. I have described the nature of those thoughts earlier. As a beginner, you may wonder if you will ever be able to just sit still, meditate, and not entertain any thought. Reaching mental clarity itself is a goal worth striving for. If you reach this state consistently, then you will find it much easier to stay focused in general. Situations you hitherto found stressful will become a lot less intimidating.

Chaos is the meditative state consisting of encountering random thoughts, no matter if you engage them or not. Whenever your mind is not occupied that way, you are in a state of clarity. As a practitioner of meditation, your goal is to minimize chaos in order to maximize its opposite, clarity. In the state of clarity, you do not engage any of the thoughts that enter your mind. Likewise, you do not actively think of something. In the state of complete clarity, your mind is empty. Aim to remain in this state for as long as possible. As an experienced practitioner, you will be able to start your meditation session in the state of clarity and never leave it until you get up and continue with your day.

Reaching mental clarity during your meditations is well and good. Furthermore, there will be certain spill-over effects into your everyday life. However, it is possible to utilize this even further if you make it a habit to calm down consciously during the day. Just by sitting still and closing your eyes for a few moments you should be able to recall this mental state and enter it as needed. The effect is even stronger if you follow certain routines for what I call mental hygiene, which I discuss later. The reason is clear, because if you distract yourself habitually, your mind does not have much of a chance to get some rest.

If you are only ever able to enter the state of clarity, you should feel perfectly content. However, a minority of you may encounter another state, which I refer to as *warmth*.

Warmth

While meditating, it is not uncommon to experience a feeling of warmth emerging from your center. It may even feel as if it emerges from your hands. This could cause psychological discomfort because it is a strange and unknown sensation. In addition to feeling warmth, you may also have the sensation of perceiving it like a physical object. To me, it feels as if a ball of energy is growing in my hands, getting bigger and bigger. Then, the warmth extends further and further, crossing my wrists, creeping up my forearms and eventually reaching the elbows. This is a clear physical sensation. You should not try to control this sensation. It is indeed possible to steer the expansion of the ball of warmth, and such can even be entertaining. However, just as learning to not manipulate your thoughts helps you reach a deeper meditative state, so will not interfering with this sensation enable you to reach an even deeper mental state by not trying to actively influence your perception.

Whenever I enter this mental state, I am not just unable to hold any thoughts; I have none appearing since my mind is too occupied processing this sensual input. I like to compare it to taking a warm bath or shower when you just stand there and let the water run over your body. You enjoy the moment and the feeling you get from the warm water touching your body. It is thus just normal that you do not waste any time thinking about anything. It is probably not that you could not, but simply that you do not want to because you do not want to spoil the experience.

After exiting this mental state, you should feel completely refreshed and at incredible ease with the world. When I meditate in the morning, the spillover effect of warmth almost makes me too unfazed. On the other hand, it is a wonderful way to end your day. Meditate for a bit, let your body get engulfed in warmth, and go to sleep afterwards. It is part of my meditative practice to remain seated in the lotus position but bend my upper body forward so that my forehead touches the ground. I remain in this position for a few minutes before getting up.

There are two levels in this state: one is the sensation of warmth in your center, which may or may not grow to reach your elbows. However, once you pass this barrier — at least I perceive it as such — you will quickly feel as if the warmth engulfs your whole body. If you manage to maintain this state, without interfering, something entirely different may happen, which I will describe next. However, let me curb your enthusiasm already as you may never move beyond feeling a warm sensation.

Unbinding

You can probably picture the effects of meditation up to the stage of reaching mental clarity. Complete mental clarity may remain elusive for quite some time. What you just read about warmth may sound odd, but presumably not crazy. At the very least you can easily imagine what this state might be like, in case you have not reached it yet. However, descriptions of deeper meditative states may sound quite strange. I cannot speak with authority on the effects of the various recreational drugs, so I am unable to confirm that the experiences through meditation are indeed drug-like. Yet, when speaking with people who are familiar with meditation and no stranger to consuming mind-altering drugs, they tend to point out the similarity.

If you lack reference experiences of deeper meditative states, the following could well be as successful as describing sex to a virgin, but I will do my best to make it descriptive. After meditating with a clear head, just letting your thoughts come and go and never engaging them, you probably semi-regularly reach a state in which the perception of yourself or your environment changes. The effect is even more pronounced if you meditate with your eyes closed as this forces you to pay more attention to other sensory perceptions. What may happen is that your perception of the boundaries of your body changes. I refer to this state as *unbinding*. You feel bigger or smaller. This can be an interesting perception to explore, but you probably tire of it quickly and return to a mode in which you do not actively engage thoughts and won't focus on this sensation either.

You probably feel resistance from the hard floor or mattress you are sitting on. Therefore, your mind might be tempted to explore this sensation further, due to a lack of alternatives. What could happen is that your mind plays a trick on you and makes you feel as if you either sink into the ground, if the underground is somewhat soft, or that you feel more connected to the hard floor, meaning that the area you are sitting on feels larger than it is. One of the most startling perceptions I had after meditating with my eyes closed was to feel as if I had sunk into the ground. I felt as if I was sitting one foot or so lower than I was. I knew that it was an impossibility and I would have lost this perception quickly had I opened my eyes, but this was not even necessary because after spending some time arguing against this obviously impossible experience, I snapped out of it. Those sensations may appear to be mere distractions, but you could also consider them a test of your newfound ability to control your mind. Just don't focus too much on them, and you may be on the way to not just superficial sensations but deeper states of meditation.

Before I go on, I would like to make a remark on the feeling of discomfort when meditating. When sitting in the lotus position, you probably feel some minor discomfort. As long as your meditation sessions are not especially long, maybe just fifteen minutes or so, this feeling may never go away. However, as you slip into deeper states, you will also stop perceiving any pain. This is only momentarily. Once the meditation is over and you open your eyes again, you quickly notice if your feet have become numb. But do not worry about your health too much. Deeper stages of meditation require significant amounts of practice. It may take years to reach them. Once you can sit for that long, you should have gotten used to meditating for prolonged periods of time, and it may even be less uncomfortable than sitting for fifteen minutes was when you were starting out.

Disconnect

Presumably, *disconnect* this is the last state. At the very least, it is the deepest state I have been able to reach during all my years of practice. You may never experience it, or only ever get a glimpse of it. It is also something I usually do not communicate. After going through a phase of feeling warmth engulfing your whole body, you may suddenly have experiences unlike anything you have had before. In fact, there are a number of possible experiences, which I am going to describe one after another. You seem to enter all of them after a somewhat lengthy period of feeling warmth.

I call it a disconnect because you will feel no connection to the real world anymore. Afterwards, you may realize that you have sat for two hours — or maybe just twenty minutes. Almost quaint, compared to the sensations I am going to describe below, are out-of-body experiences. You suddenly slip out of your body and see yourself from above, meditating. At least, that's what you are imagining. I surely do not believe that your mind exists independently of your body, thus you cannot escape it. The first time this happens, you are probably frightened by it, or maybe you are intrigued.

If you are meditating with open eyes, you may experience that the colors and shapes of objects in the room start to change and possibly bleed into each other. You may also stop hearing sounds, which is particularly startling if you are meditating in an environment that is not completely quiet. An even more extreme version of this is synesthesia, which might overwhelm you. Synesthesia is the perception of sensual data with other than the designated sensual organs. For instance, this means that you *hear* colors. Yes, I know, it sounds crazy. I do not think it is possible to describe this to someone who has not had synesthetic experiences. Apparently there are people out there that associate certain numbers with colors, but this is nothing compared to the full-blown effect you experience in deep trance-like meditation. To me, it is a complete confusion of the senses, where you feel objects on an emotional level, see noises, and hear colors. When I told some of my friends about those experiences, they told me that they sound exactly like some of their LSD trips. I have never taken LSD and do not feel like taking it to confirm this.

When reading this, you may either think that I am completely bonkers or are intrigued and want to experience this, too. However, meditation is not to be seen as a way to seek those experiences. In fact, when I enter those states, I let them happen until they either pass and I reenter the state of clarity, but more likely warmth, or until I reach a point at which I am so overwhelmed that I reflexively snap out of it.

Gateway to Serious Meditation

While those drug-like states may sound appealing, they are a distraction in the end. You will benefit most from meditation when you reach a state of calmness, which I refer to as clarity, and maintain it. With some experience, you will probably be able to enter it quickly. I can enter clarity more or less straight away. The challenge then is to not focus too much on any other experiences you may have. Yes, you may feel warmth developing in your center. Try regulating it by synchronizing it with your breathing, so that it feels as if it grows when inhaling and shrinks when exhaling. As entertaining as this may be, it is still a diversion.

Do not focus on even the warm sphere of energy

you may feel. Just let it go. Once you learn to not engage any thoughts that may pop up and likewise don't focus on any sensations you may feel, you are on the right path. By doing so, you will learn to sit for a longer amount of time and to keep your mind clear while doing so. At this level, you will also start seeing profound effects on your daily life. Your friends may even start to remark on your calmness and your ability to remain unaffected by your environment. Of course, this too depends on the kind of personality you had when you embarked on your journey of exploring meditation.

Real-Life Meditation and Mental Hygiene

As fascinating, or off-putting, as the descriptions of meditative states in the preceding chapter may have been to read, for real-life purposes, they are somewhat irrelevant. You do not meditate in order to get drug-like experiences without the financial cost of buying drugs as well as the legal risk and physical harm associated with consuming them. Reliably getting people to have LSD-like experiences without side-effects would be quite a market opportunity, though. In all seriousness, the point of meditation, for the typical Western guy, is to use it as a tool for relaxation and clearing your mind, and that is more or less it. Consistently practicing meditation, even if just for fifteen minutes a day, over many years, will have positive effects on your life. Looking back at my life, meditation has been a tool for fundamentally transforming my personality for the better.

There is a lot you can do to get more out of meditation. The most important aspect is to maintain mental hygiene. By this I mean to not expose yourself to useless information. There are many examples. To get you started: how often do you check your email or social media accounts? How often do you unlock your phone to idle away some time? Do you read any celebrity gossip sites? Do you obsess over sports? I am not saying that you cannot idle away some time every now and again. Instead, the problem is compulsive behavior, which is certainly the case with regards to the intimate relationship many people have with their smartphone.

In general, try to minimize distractions. This means, for instance, not to pointlessly multitask. Some people constantly have a video or audio source on, no matter what they may be doing. Yet, if you try to get serious work done, that kind of distraction is counter-productive. There are also visual distractions. Personally, I dislike it when my home or workplace is in disarray. If you think visual clutter does not affect you, just try cleaning up your place. You may notice a difference. Even if you think you do not care and tell yourself that you thrive on chaos: have you ever looked for something for a lot longer than you would have liked to? Also, can you see a convincing advantage of having a messy desk, room, or apartment? Even if you work in a creative field, you can surely be much more creative if everything in your surroundings is exactly where it is supposed to be.

There is also mental clutter, for instance trying to keep too many things in your head. This problem can be trivially solved by making a few notes instead of juggling your to-do list in your head. Indecisiveness is a related problem. Instead of making a decision, many people hem and haw over decisions, even sometimes rather simple ones, wasting copious amounts of time and mental energy. Just make a choice and move on!

Let us now return to meditation proper. You now know everything you need about meditation, minus the bullshit, of course. I have covered all necessary techniques and also many of the positive effects of consistent meditative practice. The latter should be motivation enough for you to keep going. At least for the first six months, focus on meditating once or twice a day and incorporate it into your daily routine, similar to brushing your teeth.

Previously, I stated that aiming for ten or fifteen minutes of daily practice is plenty of time. What I have observed in some people is a certain competitive streak that they can't seem to shake off. I used to be in the same boat as I wanted to explore for how long I could meditate. That is likewise a waste of your time as you surely have more important things to do. I suggest adding meditation to your daily rituals, but do not practice it excessively. You will get diminishing returns very quickly otherwise.

To maximize the benefits of meditation, you can, after a while, try to reach the first proper meditative state, clarity, whenever you want to or need to. Say, you have an important business meeting coming up and are getting nervous. In this case, taking the proverbial deep breath can help, but it is even more effective to spend just one minute or two in the meditative state of clarity. Of course, it can be difficult to slip into this state of mind if there is some noise or other disturbances. Even if you have your own office, it may be difficult for you because, for instance, you want to avoid to seem sleeping or daydreaming at your desk. In this case, just go to the men's room and sit down for a moment. You may come back more refreshed than you ever were. Being able to clear your mind quickly that way and regain mental clarity is beneficial in many situations. If you manage to get to that point, then, quite frankly, you can consider yourself to have graduated and stop meditating in a ritualized way altogether.

Appendix

Serious Meditation

Meditation Without Bullshit presents a simple meditative practice that can be followed by anyone. The amount of time required is rather modest. Fifteen minutes of consistent meditative practice will allow you to reap significant benefits. However, some of you may want to pursue meditation much more seriously. Only for those people have I added this appendix. Much of this information is impractical for most of you. If you have not been meditating in the lotus position for fifteen minutes for at least half a year, there is probably no point for you in even reading on.

Meditating for fifteen minutes a day can give you decent results. While it is undoubtedly true that meditating for longer will allow you to progress much faster, making that statement early in this book would make most people reflexively put it away. Obviously, it is a very hard sell to tell people to suffer physical and psychological discomfort through meditation for one hour every day, with the possibility that they may not experience much in terms of positive effects. By setting the bar lower, people are much more inclined to give meditation a try.

In the following, I assume that you are able to meditate without discomfort or with only negligible discomfort for fifteen minutes. Now that you have been meditating for a non-trivial period of time — half a year is not much in the grand scheme of things, but it certainly shows dedication — you may be eager to explore meditation further. Maybe my description of meditative states has piqued your interest. Still, your goal should not be to strive towards attaining those meditative stages. If you reach them, then let them pass you by instead of engaging with them.

For serious meditation, set aside at least one hour every day. Of course, you can as well meditate for thirty minutes for half a year as an intermediate step. Yet, the difficulty of going from fifteen minutes to one hour is not much higher than going from fifteen to thirty minutes, so you may as well go all the way. The important step is to overcome the initial state of chaos. If this takes you twenty minutes, you don't have much time left in a thirty-minute session. If you want to push yourself even further, then keep in mind that I used to meditate for two times one hour every weekday, and up to two times three hours on the weekend for years. You know when to reduce the time spent meditating once you get to the point where you can very quickly advance from chaos to clarity. If you manage to reach warmth within moments of sitting down, there probably is less of a need for you to meditate for two hours every day. Once I reached that point, I began reducing the amount of time spent meditating as well, largely based on the observation that there was no discernible benefit in longer meditation sessions with that level of experience anymore.

In particular for longer meditation sessions, it is of paramount importance to sit in the lotus position. Keep your spine straight and don't fidget. Sit completely still. I prefer lowering my chin at the start of a long meditation session as I find this more comfortable than meditating with a straight neck. The latter may lead to muscle tensions.

For a very effective meditation session, you have to reach the state of clarity as soon as possible. An experienced practitioner should be able to reach it more or less the moment he closes his eyes. Let me repeat that you should not chase the attainment of particular meditative states beyond clarity. You will commonly enter warmth and if you decide to not let go of this state, you may enter even deeper states, which are largely a distraction. I used to meditate for as long as I could stay in warmth, which sometimes caused me to end my meditation session after five to six hours as I was feeling uncomfortable. It is a very pleasant state to be in, but there is no need to explore your physiological limits. Also, those are trance-like states you may find it difficult to break out of, sometimes even with an alarm clock, as they progressively take control away from you. It is easier to snap out of them as you are slipping into those states, as opposed to when they are fully underway.

I sometimes extend the duration during which I stay in warmth by focusing on the center of the energy I feel, but I normally aim to exit this state and reenter clarity, sometimes with a detour to a deeper state. Reentering clarity after warmth happens, at least for me, with a completely empty mind. As an intermediate practitioner, you may move back and forth between chaos and clarity several times during a meditation session, while someone more experienced will not slip back into chaos.

For practical purposes, I have the impression that your biggest benefits will come from clarity and warmth. The deeper states I mentioned earlier can leave you feeling confused for a while. You may even feel drained. Consequently, I consider it counterproductive to aim for those states and try to remain in them as long as possible instead of merely passing through them.

Effects of Serious Meditation

Moderate meditation of fifteen minutes a day has a positive effect on your life. However, seriously meditating for hours a day can have a profoundly life-changing effect. I got a glimpse of that when, as a beginner, I met a monk in his fifties who had been meditating for all his adult life. The serenity he exuded was quite astounding. Consequently, I become very skeptical whenever I meet an alleged meditation guru who does not exude much calmness. It's a wide spectrum, of course, but the worst I met was an alleged guru whose body language and antics would have been more befitting of a boisterous drunkard in the corner pub.

People pick up on serenity very easily. I had complete strangers in social settings ask me why I am so calm. On a more humorous note, I have had it happen repeatedly that people in a meditation group I visited for the first time assumed that I am the teacher, or the replacement teacher, just based on how I carried myself. I have also encountered time and again that incompetent gurus were noticeably uncomfortable with my presence.

Serenity is a manifestation of being at ease with yourself and the world, which is a state you cultivate through meditation. Entering clarity will help you to some extent, but the effect of the state of warmth is much greater. The calmness that comes with this meditative state carries over into your daily life. I furthermore think that experiencing this often enough can lead to permanent changes in how you perceive the world.

In particular, meditation helped me clear up some of my neuroses. For instance, I used to have the problem that, when I was hanging out with a girl who was into me, I just couldn't make a move, for instance taking her hand or leaning in to kiss her. As much as feminists claim that it isn't so, it is a simple fact of life that attractive women only very rarely make the first move. That is your job, bucko! I had found myself in situations where I was fully aware that the girl was very interested in me. I could tell that she wanted me to touch her or that she wanted to be kissed. Yet, I could not do it. To me, it felt as if there was a barrier separating me and her. It would make for a more relatable story if I told you that I gradually chipped away at that imaginary barrier, but instead the effect was immediate and permanent. I had gotten to a point where my passivity started to bother me to such an extent that it was frequently on my mind. Yet, one fine day, after getting up from a long meditation session I had largely spent in the state of warmth, the mere thought of an invisible barrier keeping me from getting intimate with girls all of a sudden seemed ludicrous to me. From then onward, interacting with women was easy.

Let me mention one more example. The relationship I had with my father used to be a difficult one as I found him overbearing. This had the eventual consequence that I felt uneasy when he came back home from work. As soon as I heard him close the door of our house behind him, the mere knowledge of his presence started weighing on me. I do not want to insinuate that he physically abused me. That was not the case at all. Instead, he was a very authoritative father. I managed to get rid of the negative emotions associated with him by evoking memories associated with those emotions during the meditative state of chaos. My perception was that several such meditation sessions washed away the negative associations I had. Consequently, my relationship with my old man improved considerably.

I do not want you to believe that meditation is a tool that helps you solve psychological issues, although it can have that effect. To me, those are mere side-effects. Probably, this is all related to you feeling incredibly at ease with the world, which allows you to perceive imaginary problems as what they are — imaginary. Ultimately, this led to a permanent shift of my baseline level of happiness, so much so that meditation eventually turned me into a different person.

The changes I had been experiencing were of a physiological nature. Before I get to the root of this, let me tell you an anecdote. In my 20s, I once had to get an endocrinological screen during which it emerged that my serotonin levels were "disconcertingly high." The doctor said that they were way outside the regular spectrum. He told me to sit down. While he did not want to speculate, he gravely said that there is the risk that I have a brain tumor. Imagine coming home from the doctor, hearing that kind of statement! I took it quite well and mentally accepted the finiteness of my life. The next morning I got an fMRI scan. My case was seen as having high priority. No issues were found. The radiologist said that there may have been a fluke in the endocrinological screen and dryly added that he hoped his colleague hadn't soured my mood too much.

Serotonin is a neurotransmitter, which regulates your mood. To put it very crudely, it regulates your level of well-being. If your serotonin levels are high, you are in a good mood, if they are low, you are likely depressed. As I later learnt, intensive meditation has the effect of permanently raising your level of serotonin, which was what had happened with me. Through meditation I managed to increase my level of serotonin, which is the reason why I appear so calm and serene.